# Choices:
## Messages of Love to Change the Outcome

### By Bill Tortorella

Edited by: Alyn Sigworth & Justin Higgins

A special thanks to Brianna Tortorella

# Contents

1. Heaven's Zip Code  5

2. October, 1952, Ocean Parkway, Brooklyn  8

3. Twenty Five Years Later  14

4. 2003: A Human Odyssey  22

5. The Laws of God and Enlightenment  25

6. The Great Masters  28

7. The Power of Circles  30

8. Our Guides and Miracles  33

9. The Taking of Life  41

10. The Gifts and the Deeds  46

11. The Power of Love  56

12. Request the Gifts  61

13. Fears and Phobias  63

14. The Warnings  65

15. Power of Choices  73

16. Power of Lessons and Ideas  76

17. Protect Mother Earth  80

18. The Body is a Temple  82

19. A Look at Religion  86

20. Negative and Positive Pulls  89

21. Choices: Messages of Love to Help Change the Outcome  92

"For life and death are one, even as the river and sea are one. In the depth of your hopes and desires lies your silent knowledge of the beyond; And like seeds dreaming beneath the snow your heart dreams of spring. Trust the dreams, for in them is hidden the gate to eternity.

"The Prophet"
~Kahil Gibran.

# Heaven's Zip Code

For hundreds of years, science has been trying to prove that God doesn't exist. Well, that was the way they thought in the 1960's. Now, science cannot dismiss the fact that there have been so many miracles or things they can't explain. That something else exists.

What if the thing that science believes in the most, that energy created the universe is true?

Those beautiful nebulas of the universe were the heavens. It wasn't until I went to the Kennedy Space Center in May of 2009. There, my wife, kids and I were looking at some of the most beautiful pictures taken with the Hubble Telescope of Orion and the colors were so magnificent. The chills would pour through my body. The feeling of seeing that before in my near-death experience. What if the energy of the universe itself could think, feel, love and create? The energy, which force of light was the maker of all mankind; God. Could it be as simple as this? Those beautiful nebulas of the universe like Orion and eagle were the heavens. In my near death experience in 1994, that light and the love within it revealed to me the answers of all humanity from great enlightened Spirits that seemed so advanced. There is so much love and knowledge given from these great Masters. The gifts that were given to me were the nine principle Laws of Enlightenment, principles that can change our world forever.

Our home is the star dust. This is the birth place of the stars and planets. Super Nova's are exploding giant stars. They form into magnificent nebula clouds. This is where life begins, in the brilliance of its glow. These glowing forms of illumination are the enlightened ones, the great master spirits.

Carl Sagan said "Once we step into space, all laws and physics ceased to exist as we know them here on Earth".

Technology has come so far in the last 100 years. It has taken us to places we could not imagine. This is the time of choice. We have to stop and ask ourselves if all of this is right for our future. We should analyze what the outcome could bring. Let's call it for what it really is, people out of work. At this pace in forty years, the need for human contact would be gone. The jobs would follow, and then the machines will take over.

We have to create jobs. Not replace them with machines. I am not telling technology to stop, just change the direction. Replace it with machines that will create jobs, replace it with technology that will save lives.

Machines like The Reverse Life Machine, that cools the body's core down to under 50 degrees to stop brain and cell destruction. The paramedics have the technology and the time to transport. These are ides that exists today. We all as a society have to be involved. We must do our part.

Choices must be made. The battle between the light and darkness that exists today in forms of greed and bottom-line profits at any cost. Technology of the machines is moving faster than we can adjust. The jobs still exist on the lighted path of technology with machines that create instead of destroy. Light will prevail.
I invite you in to read the gift of light and love.

# October, 1952, Ocean Parkway, Brooklyn.

It's a beautiful, warm fall day. The leaves are just starting to turn. My mother relates this story to me for I am far too young to remember it. I must be about three months old. I am out for a carriage ride on Ocean Parkway. My mother sits down on a bench and chats with her friends from the neighborhood. Up the walkway she came.

She was a woman dressed entirely in black. Black lace my mother would later say. A black veil covered her face. Her black boots had ties on them. On a warm fall day in Brooklyn this must have been quite a sight. She was about to walk by the ladies when she turned around abruptly and stopped in front of my mother, "may I see the child?" she mutters.

My mother does not see any harm in this and proceeds to pull the carriage cover down. The woman begins to rub my forehead in little round circles with her thumb and the palm of her hand.

She is speaking in tongues I believe. Though my mother can speak several different languages, she has no idea what this woman is saying.

The words and the strange circling motion stop. The woman then pats my forehead and turns towards my mother. "This boy will be one of the great ones and he will do wonderful things with his life." With that, she turns and walks away. My mother never saw her again.

Years later, when I was a troublesome teen, my mother would remind me of that story. Time and time again, my mother has repeated it to me. It is now ingrained in my psyche and has become part of my history.

As a young boy, growing up in Brooklyn was a pretty amazing place. My mother, Olga, owned a bar & grill. On Franklin Avenue across the street from Ebbets Field where the Brooklyn Dodgers played. It was one of the first sports bars of those days. On game days, my mother brought me into work with her.

I was in awe. She had pictures of all the Brooklyn Dodgers around the top of the wall and they were all signed by the players. I loved baseball. It was everything to me. We had box seats right behind home plate at the ball field. After the games, the ball players would come to the bar for some drinks and food. My mom was the cook of the neighborhood. My eyes were wide open when they would come in. I remember names like Pee Wee Reese, Gil Hodges, Roy Campanella, and the manager Leo Durocher.

My mother would always tell me the story when Leo came in with a young man. He said, "The boy can't drink alcohol Olga. He's only seventeen." Mom said, "I'll give him a Coke." She asked the young man what his name was. "My name is Sandy Koufax, ma'am," he replied. I would go crazy getting those players to sign my baseball cards and baseballs.

A sad day came in 1956 when the Dodgers announced they were moving to Los Angeles. My mother was upset. We loved the game and that team. Some years went by. In March of 1963, I was in my class in school when it came over the loud speaker. President Kennedy was shot in Dallas, Texas.

I went home from school and mom and Christine were sitting at the table crying. Christine worked for us. She helped raise me as a young boy around my house. There was singing going on all the time between my mother (who was supposed to go sing with the Tommy Dorsey band) and Christine singing like ladies sing the blues. The whole block had great singers living there. Barbara Streisand lived at 460 Ocean Parkway we lived at 490 Ocean Parkway right next door. Her songs have become some of the best hits of our time.

I found a love for singing and became a singer myself. I was picked to play Tony in my schools play of Westside story. In Brooklyn on every street corner there were doo-wop groups singing. I had my group. I first listened to other groups in the different neighborhoods and learned everything I could.

There were Vito and the Salutations who sang "Unchained Melody," the Tokens that sang "The Lion Sleeps Tonight." We were still a young group singing at school dances and parties. We would sing in the hall of the train station on the intersection of Church and McDonald to get the echo. All the people came off the subway and grouped around us, tossing us coins. So the next time we brought a hat.

Years later on another afternoon, I came home and my mother and Christine were sitting at the table crying again. I asked what was wrong. Mom said Martin Luther King had been shot. This was a bad day in history.

These were changing times with the Vietnam War and Rock & Roll. The Beatles arrived in 1964 and another young man from Brooklyn by the name

David Geffen changed the music industry forever with such great Bands like the Eagels, Crosby Stills, Nash and Young and many more. And we changed to. In the neighborhood, there was a bar on one corner and a pizza shop on the other. In the bar, the men always wore flashy suits, drove Cadillacs or Lincolns. They were the mob boys. My friends and I were just the boys.

My father went on trips and told me stories of Miami, the Caribbean Islands, and Las Vegas. He was the president of one of the local teamsters unions. He brought United Parcel into teamsters when he was a young truck driver in the 1930's. He would attend and speak at conventions and tell me stories of fishing down in Florida with a friend of his, Jimmy Hoffa, and how they caught the giant king fish.

I remember one night at the house. I had just gone down to the draft board to get registered. My mother was yelling at my dad, "Don't let my boy go to Vietnam! I can't take another son's death." My older brother had just passed away a couple of years earlier from Cancer. Peter and I were very close. He was 14 years older than me and my best friend. I never heard from the draft board. I don't know what happened. I just guess my dad had some very important friends.

Just when I got my driver's license, I was approached by a man from the bar. He handed me the keys and registration to a shiny white Cadillac along with $300 to take the car from 8th street to the chop shop where they repainted them, changed the vin number, and sold them off. Brooklyn was like the Bronx Tale. That's how they recruited. I said, "Thanks, but no thanks" and handed everything back.

Choices. I already made mine and it was over the other side of the Brooklyn Bridge. I was graduating from the School of Art & Design and had other plans.

# Twenty Five Years Later

February, 1994. Tucson, Arizona.

I am attending a trade show in the Holodome at The Holiday Inn. A horrible virus breaks out and it seems like everyone is getting sick. It is a virus the health officials can't identify and we are worried it might be something like the Hantavirus. I became terribly ill. I can't even work the show. My throat is so sore and swollen that I can hardly breathe. I am full of antibiotics and medication. All I can do is lay in my hotel room and sleep.

Later on, when I talk to my doctor, he tells me that due to my sleep apnea, my throat just closed down and I stopped breathing that night. Yes, I had indeed died. Dr. Manuel Vazquez told me that several of his other patients who have died either on the operating table or on their way to the hospital and have come back have told him the exact same story.

I still remember it vividly, even today. I float out of my body through my eyes. I leave in a beautiful, glowing, fluorescent green mist. The green hue is like a fresh fern soaking in the first rays of sunshine. But it is much more than that. It is unspeakably beautiful. They say the eyes are the windows of the soul and part of the reason may be because our spirits leave our body through them and return this way too.

I hover over my body, over my bed, and I look down at myself. How cumbersome that body appears. It looks uncomfortable. I am so happy to be free. The feeling of freedom and lightness overwhelms me. The body that lies on the bed is full of pain. I feel so relieved to be out of it.

Ahead of me is a light and a tunnel. I turn towards it. What's amazing about the tunnel is that it is made up of beautiful, abundant colors. It's like when you hold up a prism to the sun and the colors just dazzle you. They are the most beautiful reds, greens, violets, blues, and yellows that you can ever imagine seeing. The intensity of these colors seem to be magnified a thousand times to me. I am entranced and pulled towards the light and those colors.

I am moving towards the light. I am moving faster and faster. I feel like I am traveling at the speed of light. The colors are whizzing by me and through me. I'm not scared. I feel nothing but protected and loved.

As I advance towards the light the love feels stronger and stronger. I feel welcomed and this feeling of love overcomes and becomes me. I am in a vast and open illuminated area. It is magnificent. Other spirits surround me and they are breathtaking. They are softer hued and misty colors. I look at them and they are communicating with me. I am communicating with them, but not in voices. I can hear myself say, in my language, in English, "Thank God I'm home." And I am home. I've been here before. I now know that I'll be there again. But for now I am home and I am joyous.

My spirit is relaxed. I can't remember my life on Earth. I don't even want to remember. All I feel and am is love. Standing here, in my spirit circle, I am bombarded with their knowledge and reasons for the meaning of life. I understand the Laws of God. I understand the purpose. I see the past and future as a whole.

I see my life now. It is shown to me. Everything good and bad I've ever done. I feel it. I relive it. The lessons I'm supposed to learn. The right and wrong choices that I've made. This is where you feel hell. It's not an afterlife. This is where you feel heaven too. Everything good you've done you will experience again. It all comes back to you in full circle.

I am standing in front of a panel of Master Spirits. They seem so advanced. There is an abundant amount of love and knowledge with this group of Masters. All the answers of the universe are within my reach. I am taking in wisdom as I stand there. One of the Master Spirits comes toward me. I feel more engulfed as more information pours in.

Next, I witnessed an amazing thing. I was invited to view events. It was almost like a giant screen opened in front of me with clips of different news reels flickering. These clips were moving so fast. It was such a real feeling. I felt I was a part of each one. I didn't know until time went by that these events were clips of our future.

It was moving so fast like the speed of a computer. I remember one of the Masters explaining a number pattern. A sequence of events linked to my life. I distinctly see my set of numbers that would alert me to many events of my lifetime. This amazed me. My set of numbers were 66. I already had events in my life related to these numbers be they good events or bad ones.

It's my own personal signal from my guides. Sometimes in one day I will see these numbers at every glance. I'll be driving and look at my speedometer and I'll be driving at 66 miles per hour. A sign on my drive shows an exit in 66 miles. I just glance at the time and it's 6:06. I turn on the radio and it's the song, "Route 66" by Nat King Cole. The numbers also appear in my dreams.

I feel this is not just for me, but also for the people I am close to or right before an important event. I usually start to see the numbers but when it also comes with a cold feeling, something bad such as a death is looming and I am ultra alert to these signs.

The first memory I have of recognizing an event with my number was when I was 17. The numbers appeared to me and it led me to draw a picture of a plane crash into a mountain. I had never felt anything like this before. Once I started drawing, it was as if my pencils were just moving by themselves across the paper. Then, what I saw on the news the following morning amazed me.

My mother and I were watching the news report about a plane that had crashed into a mountain. The flight number was the exact same number I had written on the tail of the plane in my drawing the night before. I took out the picture I had drawn from my pad and showed it to my mother and explained I had drawn it the night before. I didn't know how to feel about it at the time. Since then, I still do feel nervous when I see my number sequence but have become more accustomed to the feeling.

I have learned that the number sequences don't always represent bad events, just important ones although the accompanying feeling provides a sense of the outcome. One night after seeing these numbers during the day, I started painting a picture. I just couldn't stop. Just like when I was 17, my paint brush just flowed across the canvas. I kept painting for about a week with very little sleep. The painting was of a blonde woman walking with mountains in the background. I couldn't stop painting it once I started. It was like the paint brush was moving on its own.

After that, I felt someone of something was altering my destiny. And it did. I was about to meet the love of my life and mother of my children, Kristen. When you look at the painting, it's easy to recognize that the blond woman walking from the mountains is Kristen. She was raised in the Poconos of Pennsylvania, known for its beautiful mountains. I had painted this picture before ever setting eyes on her.

The number sequence happened again recently regarding my brother-in-law, Justin. He lives nearby and his parents were visiting from California. That night, I went to lie down to go to sleep. Suddenly, I started getting that cold, cold feeling of death around me. The whole room became cold. When my wife came to bed, I shared this with her and expressed concern that death was close and I was concerned for our family but also had a feeling that death had just happened. The next day, when I saw Justin and his parents, I learned that Justin's grandmother had passed away the night before. That night I got the cold feeling. I never met his grandmother, but because of my closeness with Justin, I picked up on the passing of his grandmother.

Be aware of your number sequence. A lot of you have them but may not have recognized it. The number events are strong alerts from our Spirit Guides. We must pay attention. Our lives are set with a path that we must follow.

I remember being told that the Principal Laws are your gifts.

"You must return," the Master Spirits said.

I recall saying, "I am home. Please don't send me back!"

"The Laws of God. The Laws of Enlightenment. You must return."

They are sending me back. Why are they sending me back? I don't want to return. I am home now. The love around me engulfs me. Please don't send me back! Suddenly, I am back in my body and I am gasping for air. I hate this sick, sick body for I can still remember the light and the love. I don't want to be here.

# 2003: A Human Odyssey

I am here and I do remember. I could divide my life into two distinct sections; before my near death experience and after. My life was altered dramatically by meeting my master guides and spirits. It was at this time that The Laws of God and Enlightenment were revealed to me.

It has taken years for me to be brave enough to tell the story. Now is the time. Both the laws and universal truths that were unveiled to me have changed my life. I believe they will change yours too. I have faith that they can change the world.

These truths are surprisingly simple and straightforward. It is said that there is no new knowledge. Knowledge is simply remembering what we've forgotten. I call on you to read and remember. I call on you to do so as I was called on to pass this knowledge to you.

We live in troubling times. Our country launched war with Al Qaeda in Iraq and other countries. The stock markets are plummeting. Huge corporations are declaring bankruptcy. People are losing faith in the nation's future. This world is being divided and broken up. These are warnings and signals that something needs to change.

This is the time to make the choices that can change the outcome of our world. If we are unwilling to change, our current methodology will bring us all to total destruction. There is a positive and negative energy that has endured throughout the ages. Living with the fear, violence, and hate that exists today is like living on the dark side. Our society is residing in a negative plateau or force field.

I will take you on a journey to the positive plane. This is a place where love rules and our spirits grow and prosper. There is an abundance of love and wealth that exists here. When we reach this plateau and the world changes the current direction it has been taking and all of humanity is saved.

Some people on earth consciously choose to be negative and they can gain followers. These are the people who would cause great harm not only to an individual but also to a whole nation of people. This is antithetical to all the Laws of God.

The one thing that we all should know is that we can control the outcome of events. We can influence the course the world is taking. It is our responsibility to do so. God's laws of enlightenment are simple and easy to follow.

# The Laws of God and Enlightenment

Simplicity reigns supreme and simplicity will save us. Nourishment and growth of the soul is directly correlated to the adherence to these basic universal principles.

### First Law: You will not and should not take anybody's life.

There are no exceptions. It is wrong to change an individual spirit's path or direction.

### Second Law: Give of the Deeds.

This means to help and give to people without asking or expecting anything in return.

### Third Law: Unleash the Power of Love.

This is to give your love fully and without reserve or question.

### Fourth Law: Request the Gifts.

Ask God to enlarge your wealth and he will enlarge your spirit.

## Fifth Law: Listen to the Warnings.
The Warnings are signs that manifest as intuition. Learn to listen and respect those voices.

## Sixth Law: Exercise the Power of Choices.
Our Spirits growth through a learning process of choice. We are given this power by God. Our spirit grows when our choices are positive in nature.

## Seventh Law: Seek the Lessons.
If you wish to become a great spirit in life you must take on as many lessons as you can. Every morning you must ask yourself what lesson will be sent to you.

## Eighth Law: Protect Mother Earth.
We need to honor and respect her. Without her, nourishment would cease to exist.

## Ninth Law: Treat Your Body as a Temple.
Take care of it. Your body has to be revered and protected for it is the vessel through which you learn and grow.

We harness the unending circle of learning and love when we bring The Laws of God into our life and consciousness. There is power in this circle.

One action begets another. There are also universal truths that exist and that we need to be aware of.

# The Great Masters

The great Master Spirits are truly the enlightened ones and the masters of our universe. Within them are all of the answers of mankind. God fuels them with the answers and the wisdom of his light. God is the light that fills us with life and his love engulfs us all.

The memory I am left with is one of complete love. I know that the time I spent with these great masters of the universe has changed my life forever. I do miss it. I know where my home is here on earth and the things I must do. But I do miss it. The feeling I had could not be explained in the form we are in. My being has become so acute to my senses and I embrace the gift that was given to me to convey. The heavens are a wondrous place of beautiful feelings, light, and love.

The Great Master that communicated with me was so wise. This master must have been thousands of years old. His light engulfed me with his wisdom. I remember vividly the teaching of enlightenment and the laws. The feeling I had that I'm finally home was so overpowering to me. I knew I belonged there. Then, when I was told that I had to return, it was by another spirit of my circle. A lighter spirit with softer hues, but brilliant beauty.

I remember not wanting to return but my life circle was not complete. My son Billy was about to be born and I had another brilliant beauty coming into my life, my daughter Brianna. I believe that the softer hued spirit I had met was Brianna and she was the spirit that sent me back here so that we could be together on earth. By the way, she was born on June 6, 2000; day 6 of the 6th month. The 66 number sequence that has been repeated again at work and impacting my life in such a beautiful way.

# The Power of Circles

"I existed from all eternity and, behold, I am here; and I shall exist till the end of time, for my being has no end."
Anthem of Humanity
~Kahil Gibran

## Circles of Life, Love, Healing, and Miracles.

Circles of life. There are no beginnings and there are no endings. Life flows like the river to the sea. The sea becomes the rain. The rain becomes the river. So it is with life. We are born into this world new again but with no beginning and no ending. Your spirit travels around with its own spirit circle. You are born. You live life to its fullest. Your body dies but you go on to build your spirit and reveal the life you have lived just to be reborn into a new life. You gain more knowledge time and time again.

Circle of love. When we become a Master Spirit, we are love. We are born with the knowledge and hopefully it stays with us throughout our life. To give love is one of God's greatest gifts. Just as in the circle, the more you give the more you'll receive. To give love is to get love in return.

Circles of Healing and Miracles. Love and faith make miracles occur. A young girl was placed on life support after a horrendous car accident. She remained in the hospital for about a week when the doctors informed her family that she would never come back. Her brain and body were dead. She exhibited no brain function whatsoever and the life support machines were the only thing making air move in and out of her lungs.

The doctor's opinion was that the girl should be removed from life support and allowed to die. The family steadfastly refused this suggestion and had the girl moved into a nursing home. Every day her whole family would circle her. They held hands and prayed over her body. They continued this ritual night and day. There is extreme power in circles of prayer. The prayer circle has no beginning or an end. It is a cycle of unbelievable energy continually encircling the person at the epicenter.

One night as the family prayed, the young girl responded with some eye movement. Then they saw her hand start to move. The family was ecstatic and called a nurse in the room. The nurse was disbelieving and thought it was just a nerve response. To the nurse's surprise and amazement, the young girl then moaned and moved some more.

What would've happened if the family had listened to those doctors? The young girl has now made a full recovery. So, miracles do occur. The family harnessed the power of circles, faith, love, and determination. Doctors have witnessed countless miracles that cannot be explained. There is a higher power. That higher power defies the laws of science and medicine.

Circles of Spirits. We all travel with our own spirit circle. Your sister may have been your mother in a previous life or your mother may have been your son. It goes on and on. You will know your spirit circle because you will gravitate to one another here on earth.

Then you will find some beings that you cannot even stand to be around. You have no interest in these people. These are spirits that are not in your spirit circle. It is not necessary to stay away from them. It is just that you will not find them to be close to you or essential for your existence and growth.

# Our Guides and Miracles

"For magic to happen in your life, you must believe in magic."
 Walk in Balance: Meditations with Lynn Andrews
~Lynn Andrews

## Our Guides and Miracles

He who seeks miracles shall find wisdom for the ones to perform miracles are God's healing hands. They are the chosen few...the miracle makers.

Miracles are near to us every day. Be open to them and they will find you. Ask for them in prayer. When we pray we actually communicate with our spirit guides. We talk to God. Prayer is our phone line into heaven.

 Since my near-death experience, I have learned that my guides assist me. They direct me and help me to make decisions. Guides are wondrous beings of light that help protect us. Some may call them angels. They are our sentries. These Masters were given their assignments by God. They walk with us every step of the way. They help us adjust our circumstances and lead us down the road that we should follow.

When you achieve the level of Guide, you have gained the full trust of God. A guide is God's spiritual worker. You don't have to look for a path. It will be there for you. Too much deliberation or vacillation is not necessary. What should be is already written for you.

Have you ever experienced déjà vu? It's the feeling that you have when you've seen or experienced something before? Déjà vu is real. You have seen it before and you have felt it before. Prior to entering this life we chose the body that we inhabit. We choose our character and our circumstances. We are shown every moment of our life before we arrive here. It's a cinematic adventure. We see our future unfold from the moment we arrive to the day we go home. I say "home" because your life in the Spirit World is your real home. Earth is just a temporary abode. It is a school of knowledge from which we graduate. We learn our lessons and then we can return home.

Home is the star dust. The beautiful nebulas of our universe like Orion and Eagle nebulas. This is the birth place of the stars and planets. Super novas are exploding giant stars that are dying. They form into giant nebula clouds of gases and dust. This is where life begins, in the brilliance of its glow. This process repeats itself over and over until it comes full circle.

What science doesn't know is that within these magnificent nebulas, there is life and knowledge that is so advanced. These glowing form of illumination are the enlightened ones. The great Spirits of our past, present, and future. I experienced a communication with those beautiful beings. That experience has changed my life.

Why would someone choose to come into this world as a blind man or a cripple? Why would someone choose a diseased or poverty-stricken existence? It's because the harder the path you select here, the stronger and faster your spirit will grow. The soul needs to reach the Master Level in the Spirit World. Those who are born with a silver spoon in their mouth will face their own challenges. Their challenge may be to share their wealth with someone who is not as financially fortunate as they might be. This does not always happen and those spirits go on living a very selfish life only to have to come back and do it again or until they get it right. They are the real unfortunates because they won't get to experience the authentic wealth that exists only in God's Kingdom. My near death experience left me with a heightened sense of feeling. I noticed this immediately. When I would meet someone and shake their hand I began to actually feel the person's spirit. I could feel the warmth and love one might have. On the other hand, I could also feel the presence of evil. It feels cold, dark, and menacing. I now sense evil very easily. One important thing I notice is a person's eyes. They become very dark in color and there is a cold feeling around them when evil lurks in their shadow. Evil is frightening. When you meet the face of evil, listen to your inner voices. Your Guides will not lead you astray.

When I said that you choose your own path here on Earth, you might wonder why someone would choose to be evil. The kinds of people who take innocent lives such as Adolf Hitler or Jeffrey Dalhmer, these are spirits that stray from the real path. Here on earth, once you are in your vessel/body, you have the freedom of choice. It is very easy to be seduced by the dark side. The negative forces can influence anyone. In most cases, our guides can keep us on the right path but the dark side is strong.

I was in downtown Los Angeles for a jewelry and watch show at the Bonaventure Hotel. At that time Los Angeles was somewhat dangerous and you had to be especially careful when the jewelry and gift shows were in town. I was on my way to join my friends for dinner. My car was parked in the lower parking lot of the hotel. It was a long, lonely ride on the escalator down to the garage.

By the time I reached the second level down on the escalator no one was around. Suddenly I heard footsteps coming up fast behind me. The footsteps stopped directly to the rear of me. It wasn't hard for me to figure out that I was in a precarious situation.

Without thinking, I turned around and jumped up one step to face the man behind me. I stood right beside him. He was extremely cold and sinister looking. He was also on drugs. He did not expect me to react the way I did. I yelled loudly, "Can I help you?" The man's eyes were as black as coal. He knew that I would fight him. I looked into those eyes and said, "You don't want to do what you were thinking."

At the same time I saw this a couple came walking in through the garage door. My would-be assailant took off running quickly out the door. I made it to my dinner that night safely. I was grateful and knew that God's guards had helped protect me.

Feelings can transcend time and space. We are connected to our Spirit Circle in ways that logic cannot explain. When I was only 17 years old, I attended the New York City High School of Art and Design. I had an after school job as a messenger for I wanted to go to Italy to study and admire the great art that originated from that country. Summer finally arrived and I was off to

Rome. I brought my art supplies with me and started sketching the city the moment I arrived. Rome was unbelievable. I was in awe when I went to Vatican City and saw Michelangelo's paintings in the Sistine Chapel. Nothing, however, prepared me for the feelings I felt when I set sight on the Pieta.

I couldn't stop looking at it. I must have spent an hour just gazing at it and marveling at the beauty and love that emanated from this work of art. For those of you who don't know, the Pieta is a statue of the Mother Mary holding Jesus after he was taken down from the cross. I was incredibly moved and spent the rest of the day drawing.

Later on that night I called home because I wanted to tell my mother about the beauty I experienced that day. When I told her about Michelangelo's Pieta, I began to get a sharp pain in the right palm of my hand. It felt like someone was sticking a spike through my palm.

The pain was intense and piercing. I did not say anything to my mother but the pain was so great that I could barely speak.

My mother said suddenly, "Billy, I have a pain in my right palm like a knife is going through it." I never told my mother that I had the same exact pain. I was young and didn't know what to think.

My mother and I were always close and we could read each other very well. Somehow we picked up this transfer of pain when I talked about Michelangelo's Pieta.

It wasn't until years later that I found out some people could actually feel the torture of Jesus' pain. I still don't know what I felt that day. All I knew was I never felt it again.

Life moves in circles. I moved to Florida and my mother and father moved to Harvey's Lake, Pennsylvania. We always had a summer home in that picturesque little town and my parents decided to move there permanently when they retired and left New York. My mother had always loved the mountains. I loved the tropics, the palm trees, and the sun.

Before my mother passed away in 1985, she told me that someday I would return to the mountains of Pennsylvania. "I don't think so," I replied. I was very happy living in Florida and never dreamt of returning to Pennsylvania.

Five years later I was still happily living in Florida when I glanced across a nightclub floor and saw the girl I knew I wanted to spend the rest of my life with. Her name was Kristen. "I think you're adorable." I said. She turned red in the face and I learned she came from the Poconos in

Pennsylvania, about a half hour's ride from Harvey's Lake.

I often think that my mother sent her to meet me. After getting married, we moved to Pennsylvania - in the same mountains that I said I would never return to. We are blessed with two beautiful children; my son Billy, who is an old, old spirit, and my daughter Brianna is grandma Olga's little girl. She acts exactly like my mother and is a constant reminder that life moves in circles and miracles do happen.

Guides are always with us. We are never alone. Trust in your feelings. Make the right choices. Love and be love. Guides are our personal escorts. We have three travel guides that stay with us throughout our lives. One is the Guide of Knowledge and Wisdom. One is the Guide of Protection and Guidance. One Guide watches over and is there to lead us on our eventual journey home.

# The Taking of Life

"No man is an island, entire of itself; every man is a piece of the continent." "Devotions", 1624
~John Donne

## The Taking of Life

You will not and should not take any person's life. There are no exceptions. It is wrong to change an individual Spirit's path or direction. By doing this you can change the outcome of one's destiny. You could have changed the outcome of our future.

It is wrong to alter the path of anyone's Spirit. That Spirit's destiny might have been an important one. All Spirits are here to set things right and take care of what they might not have taken care of on a previous journey. That is the mission of life.

Some Spirits have chosen to take the wrong path. Since you can choose your own path, you may then ask yourself, "Why would someone choose to be evil or kill innocent people?". These are spirits that stray from their real path. Once you are in your body, your vessel, you have the freedom of choice. It is very easy to be seduced by the dark side. These negative forces can influence anyone.

In most cases, our guides can keep us on the right path, but the dark side can be strong.

Sometimes money can be a catalyst to taking the wrong path. These Spirits believe that taking the wrong path can benefit them financially. They may be seduced into taking someone's life for this reason. Some spirits are drawn to the dark side. This is the negative plateau. Remember that this side can only produce negative energy. No matter how good something looks or feels, always follow your intuitions. They are never wrong and will lead you back to the light, the good and positive plane.

You do have the right to protect yourself in self-defense. You must exercise this right. No one has the right to change your path either. Hopefully, if this ever happens, you'll be able to stop the Spirit without killing them. Some people believe in revenge and follow the adage, "an eye for an eye, a tooth for tooth." They would take a life for a life. What these people don't realize is that this has accomplished nothing. All you've done is taken away the killer's misery and sent them back to another life cycle. A possible and just alternative is to lock the offender up for life with no possible access to anything.

Think about what would happen if someone took one of your parents' lives before you were born.

Maybe it is your destiny to find the cure for AIDS or something else of great importance. Every Spirit has a journey to take and we as human beings don't have the right to take it away. Whatever journey a Spirit is on is the right path for them.

Look at how the killing of President John F. Kennedy affected our destiny. We ended up staying in Vietnam ten years longer than we should have been there. One Spirit's life was taken prematurely and that in turn ended up costing thousands of additional lives.

Martin Luther King Jr. was a great man that wanted peace and equality for all mankind. He, too, was assassinated. We have no way of knowing what he may have accomplished or how our world may have changed if he was alive.

The bottom line is that killing is wrong on any level. What happens in a killing or any kind of traumatic death is that the Spirit literally jumps out of the body. The Spirit doesn't want to feel the trauma that is going to befall the body. Sometimes the Spirit will jump and stay close by to the body just to make sure the body is really dead.

This happened to a friend of mine who was in a car accident. His head hit the windshield of his car. His Spirit jumped immediately and he told me that he was outside of his body looking at his head that was face down between the steering wheel and the windshield. As soon as the paramedics arrived and started CPR, my friend's Spirit jumped back into his body. It must not have been his time to leave this earth.

This can happen when a woman has an abortion too. If a Spirit is destined to be born to a particular mother, that Spirit will stay with her. If a woman for whatever reason chooses to have an abortion, the Spirit of the unborn baby jumps. The Spirit then returns and houses itself within the mother's body until the next pregnancy occurs. The Spirit can reside within the body for some time. When the woman again becomes pregnant, the Spirit jumps back into the new baby's body. You can't kill the Spirit. The body may die but the Spirit lives on and on.

Now the spirit will house itself within the mother's body for some time but if a pregnancy does not happen again, the spirit will then leave at a further time down the line. I worked with a woman when I was living in Pennsylvania. She had told me about something that happened to her one night. She awoke from a restless sleep and as she was lying in bed, a mist came down from her belly button area. It was brilliant, bright and glowing. I stopped her and asked if it was a florescent green and she turned pale. Then I asked her if she ever had an abortion or a miscarriage. She did not answer me.

Her jaw dropped in amazement at how I could have known that she had and I went on to explain how the spirit leaves in time.

# The Gifts and the Deeds

"It's not how much we give, but how much love we put into giving."
~ Mother Theresa

## The Gifts and the Deeds

God has many wonderful gifts in store for you. Every day of your life they are there for the asking. Ask God to enlarge your wealth and he will enlarge your spirit. He will make you a better person for yourself, for your family and friends, and even for the people who are complete strangers to you. Well, you may think they are strangers, but they are not. Every encounter happens for reason. That reason may be good or bad, right or wrong, positive or negative. In a later chapter I will show you how to stay away or recognize the warnings of negative or wrong encounters, but for now, let's stay with your positive encounters. The right paths.

The positive encounters will enrich your Spirit and help it grow. This in turn makes you a happier, wiser, and more loving human being. This love will bring you riches of the heart. Now, some of you might be wondering about wealth in its monetary form. If you stay on the right path, wealth will come to you just as a river flows to the sea. Your prosperity will multiply and become immeasurable. The most important thing is for your Spirit to learn a valuable lesson and begin to ascend to a new level - a higher level of growth, achievement, and knowledge.

Gifts are there for the asking. Every day of my life I ask my Spirit Guides and God to help me to be the best I can be and to help me and bless me. Oh, do they bless you! It is not wrong to ask for the things you want in life. It is not wrong to ask for help with your work so you can make a better living for you and your family. It is not wrong to ask for anything you want in life whether it be houses, cars, boats, or even a new set of furniture.

Never be afraid to ask for as much as you want. Remember you will always have to give something back in the form of love, help, hope, and prayer. When you want something, write it down. Look at what you've written every day to remind yourself what it is that you want and what you must do to achieve it. Bear in mind that there is always some work involved. Keep in mind you must always give something back.

There are other forms of gifts and these are the most important gifts of all. They are called "The

Deeds." Deeds are gifts you give back to humanity. When we give we will receive. One doesn't just give to receive. One gives, shares, and helps in order to become a better human being. Without this exchange, life would be shallow and meaningless. Without the giving of our gifts and ourselves we would stagnate and become superficial. We would be denying the lessons of our life. We would be denying our chosen path. We would be denying our Master Guides and Spirits.

Doing a deed means to help and to give without asking or expecting anything in return. Our spirits grow when we give of ourselves without question. Deeds can be simple things like holding a door open for someone or stopping to help someone in distress.

Our world moves very quickly today and it's all too easy to feel rushed. We have to be willing to slow down sometimes if we are called upon to partake in a deed. The next time you see a car accident, slow the car down, at least ask if there's anything you can do to help. Stop, listen, and take the time. There might be a need for you to be there. Once you experience the feeling you get from doing the right thing you will begin to feel better about yourself. This is the gift that God gives you.

There are higher levels of deeds. They begin when you go out of your way to give of yourself. Volunteer work is a good example of this. You can volunteer to read to the blind ,help out in a soup kitchen, or work in a hospital. To help others in any way will create positive results in your life. This in turn helps to produce positive energy throughout the world.

There are people who make a life and a career out of the giving of gifts. These people are the Deed Masters. They are God's angels. They are the true givers.

Look at Mahatma Gandhi. By his own account, he was born a simple, shy, and fearful man. He was transformed by his personal relationship with God. Ghandi believed that "Nonviolence is the greatest force at the disposal of mankind. It is mightier than the mightiest weapon of destruction devised by the ingenuity of
man." He grew to earn the title "Mahatma" which means "Great Soul."

Think of Mother Theresa. In 1948, she found a woman who was half dead lying in front of a hospital in Calcutta. She stayed with the woman until she died. From that moment on, she dedicated the majority of her life to helping the poorest people in India. She went on to win the Nobel Peace Prize.

Consider a woman named Maria Esperanza, who founded the Betania Shrine in Venezuela where many miracles and healing take place. It is believed that the blessed Mother speaks to Maria in visions. Maria was actually able to cure a two year old boy, Ryan Hulick, of spina bifida. When you reach this level of giving, your whole life becomes devotion. These people are miracle makers and modern-day Saints.

The deed is one of the highest laws of attainable to human beings. The doing of deeds will set you down a path to the Master Level of enlightenment. We don't always plan this path. Sometimes it just happens. There is always a reason for everything although we may not be able to see the reason at that time. Some of the most important deeds in my life occurred just that way.

It was 1973 and I was doing well working in the advertising industry in New York City. I was young and naïve and decided to move to Florida only to find there was very little advertising work available there. I managed to get some freelance work but it was few and far between.

I became frustrated and started to paint pictures. I begin selling my paintings to art galleries. I made some money but I desperately needed to find a full-time job. It was then that I ran across a small classified ad looking for emergency medical technicians in the North Miami area. Although I had no experience, the ad said that they would train you for the job. I applied and was accepted.

One night at around 2 a.m., my partner and I responded to an emergency call. We arrived at the address and we were given and found the door ajar. We entered the house and from the back bedroom I heard a woman's voice. The woman's husband was lying down on the bed.

When I saw him I knew that he might be having a stroke. He could not move one side of his body and one side of his face was a little caved in. I took his blood pressure and the reading was off the charts. His pulse and respiration were both bad and he was getting much worse. His wife informed us that he wanted to go to the VA hospital. The VA hospital was over 30 minutes
away from our location. I knew the man did not have that much time and should go to North Miami General which was only about a mile from his home. When I informed his wife of this she started yelling at us and insisting that we take him to the VA.

I pulled his wife to the side and told her how bad her husband's condition was. There was no way that we should have attempted a half hour drive under the circumstances. The man overheard us and though he could barely speak, he said that he wanted to go to the VA hospital. The rule at the time was that you had to take the patient to whichever hospital they wanted to go to. Like it or not, we were on our way to the VA hospital.

By the time we got the man into the ambulance he couldn't even talk. We hadn't even driven two blocks when he went into respiratory arrest. I started an airway down his throat and started breathing for him with the Ambu bag. We still had a pulse but by the time we hit I-95, he had entered full cardiac arrest. His heart had stopped. It took us another 20 minutes to get to the VA hospital and I was doing CPR on him all the way down. Keep in mind his heart and breathing had fully stopped. For those who have never done CPR, it means you breathe for him and keep his heart pumping by hand.

He was dead for at least 30 minutes when we arrived at the VA. I was sweating profusely by this time. I kept calling his name, "Come on, George! Come on!" We brought him into the emergency room and the doctor came in, felt his pulse, and found nothing. He walked away. I continued to perform CPR on him and kept calling out his name saying, "Come on, George!"

All of a sudden I felt his heart start up. I knew he had a pulse. I said, "Doc, he's got a pulse!" The doctor pulled me back and put his stethoscope on the man's chest. He turned to me and smiled, saying, "Boys, he's back!" The feeling that I had overwhelmed me. It felt wonderful that I could help that man. A deed makes an imprint on your soul that lasts forever.

I'll never forget the night my partner and I responded to a call for an emergency car accident. When we arrived at the scene it was apparent that the accident was very bad. I hopped out of the unit and saw young man crying, "My sister, my sister, help her!" I ran over to the car and saw that his sister's head had gone through the front window. Half of her head was on the inside of the window and the other half was on the outside. I thought that she might be dead but just then I saw a small movement from her arm. My partner and I rushed to pull her off of the window. The glass was at least six inches back into her head but we finally got her free. I could see some breathing in the girl but there was blood everywhere. Whenever there is a head injury, it bleeds profusely. At that time we put her on a backboard and I started trying to apply bandages to her head.

We then got her into the unit. No sooner had we got her in when her whole body started jumping up and down. She was in a very bad state of shock. It reminded me of a seizure. I tried to hold her down. I had her head between my arms and my hands

were holding down the top of her head with gauze pads.
I could not hold her legs. Her brother was in the back of the unit with me. He was looking out the back window crying. I yelled out, "God help me!" Her body was thrashing so hard that I told her brother to get up and sit on her legs so I could try to hold on the bandages.

Thank God we were only a few minutes from Parkway General Hospital. We arrived at the hospital a few minutes later. We got her in the emergency room. I had a lot of hope and prayed for that young girl. She was only about eighteen years old but she had lost so much blood and she was still unconscious when they ran her off to surgery.

Our job was done there. My partner and I left to go to our station to shower and get a new change of clothes. When an accident is that horrific, it's hard to stop thinking about it. The whole day I reflected on that girl and prayed for her. Very rarely do you even want to go back to ask the hospital what happened because when it's that bad most of the time the outcome is bad too.

But the next morning I felt like I had to go back to the hospital to find out. I went into the emergency room to ask what had happened to that young girl we brought in yesterday morning. One of the nurses I knew was on duty. She said, "Why don't you go up to her room and introduce yourself?" "She's still alive? I answered." The nurse replied, "I will take you up to meet her."

I was in shock. My whole body filled with happiness for her. When we got to her room, she was sitting up in bed. Her brother ran over to me and hugged me and introduced me to his sister, "This is the man that saved your life," he said.  She was so happy and may I add, so lucky. I think God was listening to me when I yelled out, "God help me!" The young girl, Carol, did not have any brain damage at all. I left the hospital feeling wonderful about the gift that God gave me to give back. Pay attention in your life and look for the gifts that God will give you to return to others. Ask and ye shall be given. Seek and ye shall find. Live fully and love freely. Your Spirit Guides will bless you and life will again become wondrous.

# The Power of Love

"Love is a sacred reserve of energy; it is like the blood of spiritual evolution." ~ Pierre Teilhard de Chardin.

## The Power of Love

When we pass over into the spirit world we are totally engulfed in a sea of love. This love is like the air that you breathe. It becomes part of you and your total existence. It is the highest level that we can attain here on earth. It is the most important thing there is. When you love fully and fearlessly, without reserve or question, you are free to become a Master Spirit in the spiritual world. The Masters are the noble ones. They are Kings and Queens in the eyes of God. Master Spirits come with abundant amounts of knowledge. The knowledge they possess is God's greatest gift to us.

You may feel that this kind of love is impossible to achieve but nothing could be further from the truth. It is simple in its form and essence. God has given us all the tools to work with. All we have to do is pick them up and use them.

Begin by thinking about what the word "love" means to you. Is it a feeling you have for another person or for your job? Dig a little deeper and you'll discover that love is everything in one's life.

Love is part of your inner soul. For you to achieve love all you have to do is be love. Learn to use love every day. Love is found in a gesture. Love manifests itself as a respect for all living things. Love is a reverence for life.

All the great ones, the Master Spirits, have been around for thousands and thousands of years. Master Spirits have attained this level of love. Look at the real meanings of Jesus' teachings. We are one and love is all. To become love all we have to do is practice love. When humans listen to the great masters of the world, they begin to understand the real meaning of life.

It's not important who has the most money, or the biggest house, or the best job, or even which country will control the oil reserves. What's important is whom we love and who loves us. What's important is what we give back and not what we take. Giving back can be a small activity, like a smile to a stranger. Giving back can also be a huge undertaking like trying to find a cure for cancer.

Let's start with the smile. This is a gift that's easy to give. You will find that if you smile a lot you begin to transfer your love. You feel better in your heart because when you are smiling it's impossible for negative feelings to exist. If you don't believe, me try it - smile. Now attempt to feel bad or depressed without taking the smile off your face. It's just not possible to do because a smile is a transfer of love. Smile at the world and you will feel better each and every day.

There is a ladder of love. To take the next step you can combine a gesture with a smile. It's simple. Help someone with a chore without asking for anything in return. Help someone in distress. If someone asks for your assistance, be it family, friend, or stranger, don't hesitate. Just help. Love is more than just your thoughts. It's your actions. This may involve a little work but it will make your spirit grow in leaps and bounds. Once you start to practice this you will find you want to do it again and again.

You climb one more rung when you learn to share. Sharing helps you to grow because when you share, selflessness cannot exist. To be selfish in your life will slow your level of elevation down. Sharing is a gesture of love. The more we give the more we will receive.

Do not worry too much about money. Money is nice to have but it will not make your spirit grow. It is not wrong to make money as long as you don't take advantage of someone else. The object of money is to improve the quality of your life and other people's lives.

You are nearing the top of the ladder now - true love. This is the gift of love that marriage celebrates. It is the gift of love that you give to yourself and someone special. Open your heart and give freely and without reserve. Give without expecting anything in return. Be there for each other's problems. Nurture and respect one another. If you do this without hesitation you will achieve and maintain this level of love.

Love teaches you forgiveness. Learn to release and forgive. Don't throw stones at one another. Forgiveness is a love in itself. If you can't learn to forgive one another your relationship will deteriorate. God does not judge this way and we in turn do not have the right to judge another human being. Forgiveness is an undertaking on the road to enlightenment.

When two like-minded souls combine their energy and work together in harmony they create a third energy. This energy is powerful and is the gateway to the universe. Love begets love. Love of all humanity and nature begins with the correct loving of one human being. True love can transform you. True love can open doors and take you to heights that you never thought possible.

We have climbed to the top of the ladder. What do you see? One of the highest forms of love, and one we frequently overlook, is the love of Mother

Earth. We need to honor and respect her. She is a wonderful spirit. She is our home. She lives and breathes and gives us life. We must take her hand and shelter her from storm. Without her, nourishment we would cease to exist.

On a nice summer day, I invite you to take a walk with her. I promise you if you do that you will never look at a plant, a tree, or a flower in the same way again. Stop to admire the flower. Breathe in its scent. Feel its petals. Ask yourself how it was made. It was created from the love that she gives. We are fortunate to have this beautiful earth on which we can live and thereby reap the knowledge that is necessary to help our spirits grow. We are lucky to live so we can learn to love.

# Request the Gifts

"Prayer is not an old woman's idle amusement. Properly understood and applied, it is the most potent instrument of action."
~ Mahatma Gandhi

## Request the Gifts

Ask God to enlarge your wealth and he will enlarge your Spirit. Again, it is not wrong to ask God for the things in life that you desire as long as what you ask for does not harm anyone in return. Remember, you must always give back in order to receive.

I ask and speak to my Spirit Guides every day. The way to contact your Spirit Guides is through prayer. I pray with my heart and soul. My hands are placed together with my thumbs and my fingers. I point them up towards the heavens and cover my eyes. I ask my Spirit Guides and Masters to help me with everything I do throughout the day. I ask for exactly what I want to achieve. You must be direct and clear with your requests. They will listen to you. I often think of this as my direct phone line to God.

If you are in a sales job, ask for help in achieving your sale that day. If you ask you shall receive.

You can repeat your prayers over and over. It is important to acknowledge and thank your Spirit Guides and Masters for their help. The gifts are there for the asking. God wants you to receive them.

God will enlarge your Spirit through his reservoir of knowledge. God will let you know if your requests are the right path for you. You must remember that if something was meant to be, it will be. The knowledge that God gives you is one of the greatest and most wonderful gifts of all. He who asks for God's love and blessing shall always receive it.

# Fears and Phobias

The great Spirits of enlightenment that showed me that hall of events also gave me knowledge about my fears and phobias. When I was younger, I had a tremendous fear of snakes. When I would see them up close I would always have a bad feeling and be terrified of them. I'd often have nightmares about snakes. I remember that the Great Spirit told me that my fears are not what they appear to be. My fear has nothing to do with snakes. It has to do with future events related to my health.

Over the past few years, I've been suffering from lower back pain. In November of 2011, I had surgery to repair damaged discs I had in my spine and the doctors said it would help but 3 months later that pain was back and even worse than it was before the surgery. I then realized that the snakes I was so terrified by as a youth represented spinal cord injuries. I'm no longer terrified by snakes as an adult.

Some of you may suffer from a fear of heights, water or drowning, fire, close quarters, even talking to people. The thing you must know is that that you are afraid of is not real. The fear does not stem from the focus of your fears, but what those fears represent. Once you realize this that is the first step in overcoming your fear or phobia.

People are nervous or anxious about things that do not exist. Its one thing to be nervous if you did something wrong but it's another thing to have panic attacks over a feeling. Some of you know exactly what I mean. Your heart races and you are afraid but don't know why. The Master Spirits told me that they are warnings of future events. These are warnings to help keep you on your path. When this happens, I want you to say the Prayer of Jabez. Say it over and over. Ask God for His blessing. Ask for exactly what you want such as to feel better. Then ask Him to enlarge your territory so you could pass His blessing on to others. Once you start doing for and focusing on others through acts of service, the panic will subside and fade away. Next, ask God to touch you with His hand, same as His love. Lastly, ask God to keep you from evil or doing evil. Say it as the exact prayer or like this over and over.

God will bless you later on down your path. You will find out in time what the real problem was. What the fear or phobia really stemmed from. Remember that your prayers are your phone line to the heavens.

# The Warnings

"The more faithfully you listen to the voice within you, the better you will hear what is sounding outside. And only he who listens can speak."
~ Dag Hammarskjold

## The Warnings

The warnings are signals from your Spirit Guides. We are always being watched. You are never alone. We are looked after from the moment we arrive until the moment when we go home. Everything is planned out for us. These warnings are signs that manifest as intuition. We are warned what direction we should take. We are warned by feeling when something is wrong. We all have Spirits guiding us. Learn to listen and respect those voices.

A whisper in your ear is an invitation to move towards the path of light. Never let anger steer you in a negative direction. Even if someone tries to hurt you, it doesn't matter. The only ones they will hurt are themselves. This is because of life's circles. It's a common saying that what goes around, comes around. This is true. The type of people who would try to hurt you are at the lowest level of that the spiritual realm.

Nothing good can ever come from anger, fear, or hate. Actually, these feelings cannot exist when love is present. Also remember that nothing happens by accident and everything happens for a reason.

Listen to the warnings and they will guide you. I vividly remember a day many years ago in North Miami Beach. My son, Joey, was only about five years old. Joey was on the edge of a canal throwing bread to some hungry ducks. I stood behind him and watched.

Now, I am very comfortable around water. I love to swim, snorkel, and scuba dive. Suddenly, something told me to pull Joey back to where I was standing. This feeling made absolutely no sense. The water wasn't deep, so there was no reason for me to feel that Joey might be in danger. My intuition was warning me to get Joey out of there.

Thank God I listened. I pulled Joey back and less than a minute later, a 9-foot alligator lunged out of the water. It happened so fast that I didn't see it coming. The alligator grabbed one of those big ducks in his mouth and then just slid back into the water and disappeared. If I did not listen to the warning it might've been my son.

In 1988 I was on a business trip to the Orient. I ignored a warning there and it almost cost me my life. My ex-wife, Bernadette and I were on a buying trip to Korea, Hong Kong, and China. We had been having a wonderful stay and had seen many unusual and amazing sites.

The last leg of our journey took us to Bangkok, Thailand. We went there to meet with some marquisate jewelry manufacturers. When we landed at the airport, government tourism guides greeted us. We decided to set up some tours. Bernadette and I wanted to visit the Buddhist temples, the Grand Palace and partake in the 007 boat ride. We passed through customs and I declared a substantial amount of money and jewelry that I had on my possession.

On the way to our hotel, I started to get an uncomfortable feeling. It was a strange feeling that I had never had before. I was not as conscious of warnings at this time in my life and did not recognize the feeling. I let it pass.

The first day of business went fine. I forgot about the feeling and the next day we embarked upon our tours. A guide accompanied us the whole day. At the Grand Palace we had to remove our shoes and place them in a bin. It was early afternoon when we finished up.

I went to find my Reebok sneakers and discovered that they were missing.

A Thai guard came running up to me and said, "Your Reeboks, your Reeboks." He had us follow him into the guard house in the Palace. When we entered the room my sneakers were on the floor. A Thai man was bowing up and down and speaking in Thai. The guard explained to our guide that the man had stolen my shoes and must be punished.

The guards were acting like this was a serious crime. I found out later that to commit a crime in the Grand Palace is punishable by imprisonment. I told my guide to tell them that we would like to leave and to please let the thief go. "He can't leave and the American can't leave", they replied to my guide.

"We are required to file a report with the tourism police station and the thief must be punished."

They urged my guide and Bernadette to leave and said that they would take me back to my hotel. Lucky for me, Bernadette and my guide refused.

About an hour later an unmarked car pulled up. Out stepped a Thai soldier and an Australian man who reminded me of James Bond.

"What is going on?!" I demanded. "We're visiting your country and now we're being held up." The Australian man told me he was taking me to the tourism police station to sign some papers. They again tried to separate me from my wife and guide by urging them to go. They both refused to leave me behind.

We all got into their car and drove through Bangkok until we reached the outskirts of the city. Instead of a police station, what they took me to was a house. I had a very, very bad feeling by then. The house had no furniture. There was only a desk with a light above it and a couple of chairs. Guards with machine guns guarded the entryways.

The thief was carted off to another room and they started questioning me, "Why are you in Bangkok?"

My guide told us she thought that this was normal procedure but I knew something was definitely wrong. I started to get up to leave and a Thai guard came over with a machine gun. He hit me with his gun and then pushed me down with the gun flat on my back. Bernadette started to cry. They kept asking me how much money and jewelry I had. They again told Bernadette and my guide that they should leave.

At this point our guide started yelling at them in Thai while we stood there in silence. A man entered the room with a stack of papers and said, "You sign, you sign."

I asked to call the US Embassy. The last thing I wanted to do was endorse papers in a language I couldn't read or understand. My guide looked into my eyes and said, "Bill, trust me. I will read every page and translate into English." I looked back into her eyes and I believed her.

My guide read the papers. She said they were all about the man stealing the sneakers in the Grand Palace. At this point, she knew something was wrong too. I signed the papers and my tour guide started arguing with the men. She turned to me and whispered, "Bill, I want you and your wife to get up and walk to the door as quickly as possible." The guide was yelling at the men and they were yelling at her. "My driver is just down the block" she said.
Bernadette and I walked quickly out the door and our guide followed us.

We ran into our car and the guards were still outside yelling as we sped away. All the way back to the hotel the guide kept apologizing for her country. I had come to the conclusion the reason why they wanted to separate us was to shake me down for money and my gold Rolex watch. The guide agreed with me. Thank God she and Bernadette refused to leave me that day.

When we got back to the hotel we still had the feeling they might come back for us any time. I immediately got on the phone and tried to book the next flight out of Bangkok. It took a while and cost me $3,500.00 but we were able to catch a 5 a.m. flight to Japan then onto to the United States. We had a definite feeling we should leave and this time I was wise enough to heed the warning. It took three days for Bernadette and I to stop shaking.

Intuition is not to be ignored. The results can be dramatic if you do. Intuition is a gift from our Spirit Guides. It will guide you in the direction you need to follow. Learn to listen. Warnings speak your name. They are your earthly guidance.

Warnings pave a trail that you should follow. When you veer off the path it can be dark and scary. That territory is unmarked. It's easy to become lost. Listen to your inner voices and you need never fear.

The heart and soul have their own music and rhythm. Our logic cannot comprehend the sounds. The echoes from our Guides should never be dismissed like the wave of a hand. They reverberate through all eternity. They are the sounds of God.

# Power of Choices

"Events, circumstances, etc. have their origin in ourselves. They spring from seeds which we have sown."
~ Henry David Thoreau

## Power of Choices

Our Spirits grow through a learning process of choice. We gain knowledge by our mistakes and our Spirit grows and prospers. The choice is always ours. God gives us this power. When the spirit chooses the right path it has completed a lesson. God gave us wisdom so we could determine the difference between right and wrong.

We are all paintings of our own soul. We are voices from our past, present, and future. Our life is a statement about the choices we have made, be they positive or negative. Our state of life and our happiness stands in direct proportion to the type of thoughts we've chosen to engage in and our belief system.

Whatever happens in our life, good or bad, is a direct result of the choices we have made and the thought processes we have chosen to undertake. There are no accidents in our life. We are not victims of circumstance. If we are victims it's only because we've chosen to be.

We choose our life. We choose our destiny. We can choose to be noble. We can choose to rise above. We can choose the only choice there is and that is to be one with the Universe, to be one with ourselves, to be one with God and all mankind.

If you do harm to another, the harm comes back to you. In reality you only harm yourself. It does no good to hate or to fear. It does no good to seek revenge. In reality there is no revenge except upon oneself.

Life is a canvas with lessons to be learned. Be alert for those lessons and have your paintbrush ready. Open your mind and open your heart. When you do you shall see the colors appear before you with a magnificent stroke of inspiration.

Our spirit grows when we are on the right path. There is a great force in the universe of both positive and negative energy. For our spirit to grow we have to stay on the positive plane. A negative alliance might seem very appealing or an easy way out but this will never help our spirits grow. It only sets us back. Remember that it's always possible to change directions. Sometimes it's hard to tell the difference between right and wrong. We must rely on our instincts or what we call intuition. This intuition is a message from our

Spirit Guides leading us down a trail we need to ponder.

If you listen to your heart and soul it will never lead you astray. Intuition is the touchstone of God. Learn to hear his whispers and you will follow them. When you tune yourself to the sounds you will live as lightly and as freely as the wind that blows through the leaves of the willow tree. Your heart will soar and you shall receive whatever it is that you ask.

# Power of Lessons and Ideas

"Live as if you were to die tomorrow. Learn as if you were to live forever."
~ Mahatma Gandhi

## Power of Lessons and Ideas

All steps we take in life are lessons. If you wish to become a great spirit in life you must take on as many lessons as you possibly can. Every morning you should ask yourself, "What lesson will be sent to me today?"

Lessons are sent to help expose us to new territories and open up our boundaries. One must take new and different chances whenever possible. You must learn to move beyond your comfort zone. If you feed on your ideas, your ideas will become your reality.

God gives you many chances each and every day. All you have to do is look for these chances and apply them. Any idea is a good idea but ideas involve implementation. You have to work on them. Don't just let your idea fade away. The best way for you to achieve this is to write down all of your ideas and then begin to work on the ones that really move you.

After my reunion with God I came back feeling very close and connected to my Spirit Guides or, as some might say, the angels who watch over me, protect me, and guide me. I started listening to my inner voices and I started paying attention to my ideas. Since then I've found that nighttime is when I am most in touch with the other side.

One night, at the time of my life when I was in the jewelry and watch business, an idea came to me. The idea was to put angels on watches. At the time this hadn't been done before. The first thing I did when I awoke in the morning was to write my idea down. The next thing I did was to actually visualize my idea. I started drawing pictures of angels on watches. When this was done I took action. I brought my pictures to one of my jewelry manufacturers. Within two to three weeks of that moment I had my hand drawn samples manufactured and ready for sale. Only one month after that I received an order from QVC for over 10,000 pieces of my angel watches. By the way, the first order sold out in less than 20 minutes of its television preview.

This concept works fast if you allow it to. Listen to your inner voices and follow them. Take every idea that comes to you as the gift that it was intended to be. Your ideas are your opportunities. Write down your idea, visualize it, and act upon it. The world will be given to those who desire it and are willing to take the action necessary to achieve it. An idea is an opening. Anything is possible if you listen, believe, and are willing to work at it.

This is a universal truth or law. Before I understood this concept consciously, I can still see how it worked in my life. When I was only eighteen years old I lived in Brooklyn, New York and was a student at the School of Art and Design. One day, as I listened to our local radio station; WABC, I became excited to learn that they were sponsoring a contest to promote the new musical "Jesus Christ Superstar." The contest was to design a card in celebration of the musical. Three winners would be chosen; one for the largest card, one for the smallest card, and one for the most artistic card.

That night my mind started to race. I couldn't wait to get started. The next morning I was in a lumber yard and came home dragging two 4 foot by 8 foot plywood boards and a set of hinges. My mother saw me as I came through the door and shook her head as she said, "Billy, what are you going to do now?"

Well, what I was going to do was paint my picture. In my mind I could already see Jesus Christ,

standing seven feet high, with his arms spread out in love. Hundreds of people were behind him holding crosses and torches as they fled their burning town on top of the mountain. As they reached the bottom of the mountain they reached out for Jesus' love and he gave it to them.
I had no way of knowing there would be over 250,000 contestants in that contest nor did I care. I was drawn to enter and ended up winning in the category of "most artistic card."

Ideas are a gift from God. Lessons are also a gift from God. Just open your heart and let them in. They will come. Have faith and God will steer you in the direction you need to go.

Too often we close our hearts, souls, and minds to the gifts and new experiences that are being offered to us. To turn our backs on these gifts is to close our spirit and soul to the growth process that is our birthright and is our mission.

We are brought to earth to love, learn, and to become better human beings. We all have lessons to learn and if you will listen carefully and trust, these lessons will present themselves to you. Remember to work on these lessons. Do not let something as important as a gift from God fade away.

# Protect Mother Earth

"This we know: the earth does not belong to man, man belongs to the earth. All things are connected like the blood that unites us all. Man did not weave the web of life, he is merely a strand in it. Whatever he does to the web, he does to himself."
The Power of Myth
by Joseph Campbell with Bill Moyers
~ attributed to Chief Seattle

## Protect Mother Earth

Mother Earth is the Spirit that gives us life. She is our heart and soul. She is the birth mother of humanity. Her influence extends from the plants and trees that provide us with oxygen to the vast supply of water that nourishes us and makes all living things grow. She is the jugular vein of our existence. We must protect her and she in turn will protect us and give us life.

Our earth is a marvelous place to live. When you stop to consider the beauty here it's amazing. The majesty of the mountains, the bounty of the planes, the turbulent and tempestuous ocean. When we accept Mother Earth as one of the Great Spirits we will come to understand what makes us one with the earth.

Stop to marvel at the miracles she creates every day. Take a look at the food that's on your kitchen table. Mother Earth supplies It. The water we drink is her offspring. The air we breathe comes directly from her nostrils. She is the entity we draw our life's breath from.

She takes care of us and the entire kingdom of animals. There is a place for everyone and everything here. She's here to help supply us with a bountiful life, so be careful with any abuse done to her. She is not just ours for the taking. What we remove from her body we must replace. The same applies to the animal kingdom. Do not destroy what will not be used for food. Remember every animal also has its own Spirit and path to follow.

Listen to her wind. Her voice will speak of higher places of enlightenment. Watch her rivers flow and you will know that this is her strength that is flowing into the sea. Picture yourself as an angel and glide above the mountain peaks and plains. Across the vast and beautiful oceans you will come to feel that you are one with the earth and the earth is one with you. Love her and respect her for she holds the voice of reason that we must obey and honor.

# The Body is a Temple

"I sing the body electric."
~ Walt Whitman

## The Body is a Temple

Your body is your temple. God does not want us to damage our body in any way. It's a vessel that we sail from birth. The idea is to be able to maximize its use for as long as possible. We treat our bodies well so we can prolong the time period that we're here to learn. Every minute that we spend on earth helps our spirits grow. Destroying our body with drugs, alcohol, cigarettes, or mutilation is not only unhealthy - it's an abomination.

This is one of God's laws. Keep the body temple so it can take you on your journey. Your vehicle, your body, can take you to amazing places. You can choose to steer your vehicle in many different directions but you need to keep it in the best condition possible.

When I was younger I sometimes would put my body at risk by being abusive to it. Like my other teenage friends, I experimented with alcohol and drugs. When I started to see my friends overdosing and killing themselves, I began to wake up and consider the consequences. I can't count the number of funerals I went to. Thank goodness I never tried any hard drugs like heroin. I've seen it destroy so many lives. It's a drug that will lead you to only one of four scenarios; jail, hospital, a mental institution, and ultimately death.

Some people are overly concerned with their body image. There are many people who will starve themselves just because they think it will make them more attractive. It is possible to become anorexic or bulimic in pursuit of the ideal body. Unfortunately, this can be very detrimental physically and even result in death in severe cases. Above all else, we should always remember that it's a person's inner beauty that's really important. True beauty radiates from our soul.

On the other side, we can find people who eat themselves to death. Some people eat to be happy. Some people eat when they are bored. Some will eat food just because it's there. My advice on this is simple. The only reason to eat is if you're hungry. Food is there to nourish us, to give us energy.

I can understand obsessions with food because I love to eat. I am a lover of great food. It's a wonderful feeling to enjoy a delicious meal. If you're like me, just watch the size of your portions. The body is the vessel that we live in. Keep it, use it, love it, and respect it. It will take you on God's journey to all the wondrous places your spirit will seek. There is never any reason to feel insecure about one's temple. No matter what you look like or what shape you're in, God loves you. Remember, your body is just a vessel.

It's also important that we keep our bodies from harm for the sake of our children. We should be there to hug them, squeeze them, and tell them we love them each and every day. It's so important to their life if they are to become well-adjusted. You are your children's leader. You're their shepherd and there your herd. You have to lead them down the right path and send them off in the right direction.

I recently watched a documentary on television titled Homeless to Harvard about a remarkable woman named Elizabeth Murray. I was mesmerized by what an amazing spirit this girl had. She's a wonderful example of what positive choices can do for you. This girl had all the odds stacked against her from the time of her birth. Her mother and father were both drug addicts. She was bagging groceries at eight years old to make a few dollars so the family could eat. This was a little girl who always took care of her mother rather than being taken care of.

Elizabeth's mother and father got infected with the AIDS virus. She was left homeless and wandering through the streets. The only life she ever knew was struggle and despair. Her mother died and her father ended up in a homeless shelter. Elizabeth was left to grow up pretty much on her own.

Her amazing Spirit chose to pursue the positive side of life. Although she was a dropout, she returned to school and earned her high school diploma in only two years. At night, she slept on the subway trains. It wasn't easy, but her spirit was focused towards the positive directions necessary to get her out of the situation she was born into. Elizabeth moved on and became the winner of the New York Times Scholarship Award. She then attended Harvard University.

Elizabeth made the right choices. She is a wonderful example of positive energy and motivation. Her story illustrates how strong the human spirit can actually be and how much it can overcome. The body as a temple must be kept clean if it is to accomplish what it needs to on this earth. The body must be healthy so it's free to complete the circle of life.

# A Look at Religion

"This is my simple religion. There is no need for temples; no need for complicated philosophy. Our own brain, our own heart is our temple; the philosophy is kindness."
~ Dalai Lama

## A Look at Religion

Almost all religions have the same concept. This is the idea that there is only one God. But religions sometimes twist the basic premise. And that is the principle of Love. Love is the true religion. God is in all of us. We are all God's children. We are one. God does not say that one religion is better than another. All you really have to know and feel is that God is love. So the basic foundation of religion, the love, is your true path in life. Human beings distort religions. Why do we believe that a priest has to practice celibacy? It's a perversion that a human being is not able to marry or feel love. It's not even humane to ask. This is not a belief that arose from Jesus' teachings. Jesus never requested that his apostles not marry. The church developed these theories.

The idea of purgatory was an invention of the church. Do you think that is what Jesus wanted for us? That we make up rules that fit our purposes? Jesus was love. He was pure, unadulterated love.

Jesus shared his love with humanity. I believe that the basic values inherent in all religions are in accord and genuine.

Like Dr. Brian Weiss said in his book Many Lives Many Masters about Christianity, Buddhism, Hinduism, and Judaism:
"Christianity is wonderful if you follow the right path. Love fully and God will render every man according to his deeds. If you forgive others for the wrong they have done, your heavenly father will forgive you and pass no judgment. You will not be judged. Do not be concerned with storing up treasure on earth. Work on storing up treasure in heaven. God is love and he who abides in love abides in God and God is with him.

Buddhism conveys a great respect for all living things. It is a law of the universe that as we sow, so we shall reap. Hate is never diminished by hatred. It is only diminished by love. This is an eternal law. You reap the things you have sown. The heart of this law is love. The end of it is peace.

Hinduism beliefs are that the noble-minded dedicate themselves to the promotion of peace and happiness of others. This is the sum of all true righteousness. Treat others as you would like to be treated. Seek the wisdom by doing service, by strong search, by questions, and by humility. Say what is true. Do your duty. Do not swerve from the truth. Do not hurt others.

Judaism is a very family-oriented religion that feels the most beautiful thing a man can do is to forgive wrong. Thou shall love thy neighbor as thyself. What is hurtful to yourself, do not inflict upon your fellow man. Judge not your neighbor until you are in his place. A liberal man will be enriched and one who waters will himself be watered."

Are these religions really so different? When we realize that we are not separate entities and are all part of an unbroken circle of energy, we will truly grow to enlightenment. By being one with the world we also help ourselves to grow and prosper.

**The Prayer of Jabez**

**"Oh that you would bless me indeed and enlarge my territory. That your hand would be with me, and that you would keep me from evil. That I may not cause pain!"1 Chronicles 4:9-10.**

# Negative and Positive Pulls

"When bad men combine, the good must associate; else they will fall one by one, an unpi2003tied sacrifice in a contemptible struggle."
Thoughts on the Cause of Present Discontents, 1770
~ Edmund Burke

## Negative and Positive Pulls

Everything in our universe is made up of energy. This energy is the basis of the universe. It is our life force. The energy around us is either positive or negative. Negative energy creates negative energy and positive energy creates more positive energy.

The earth itself responds to negative or positive forces or pulls. When there is a disturbance in our force it is because there are too many destructive acts being committed by a large number of people. Negativity breeds negativity and calamity. Positive acts, kindness, and love breed a positive and peaceful planet.

Prior to the war in Iraq and at the beginning of it, I would wake up every night drenched in a cold sweat. I suffered repeated dreams of tornadoes hitting our country with a massive force. I told my family about these dreams but they did not abate. I have since realized that my dreams foreshadowed the beginning of a negative pull that currently exists on our planet.

Today, I heard on the news that over 300 tornadoes occurred this week and caused massive destruction across the world. Since the time of the outbreak of the war in Iraq we have also experienced an outbreak of the SARS virus. So far this insidious virus has killed hundreds of people.

This is a negative outcome in direct response to a negative action. Any killing of any kind breeds a negative reaction. A war that winds up causing thousands of deaths is devastating to our planet. Any action, whether positive or negative, will breed an equal reaction. This is what we're seeing now.

Negative pulls can be redirected into positive pulls and we as individuals and as a society must be aware of this and begin to act upon it. We can alter the disturbances that exist by engaging in positive actions. It is not too late but we must act at once. Humanitarian aid and good deeds need to commence immediately.

Any destruction that occurred must be rectified and rebuilt. Families will need to be put back together. Imagine if we took just half the money that is spent on war and use that money for health care, education, and food for the hungry. We would begin to heal the world and gain respect and friendship instead of animosity and adversity. This is an example of a positive energy pull. A positive action will breed a positive reaction. To love and to give is to be one with God. God is with us all.

# Choices: Messages of Love to Help Change the Outcome

"Darkness cannot drive out darkness. Only light can do that. Hate cannot drive out hate. Only love can do that."
~ Martin Luther King Jr.

## Choices: Messages of Love to Help Change the Outcome

Ultimately we have important choices to make in our immediate future. The choices we make as individuals will shape and change the destiny of our world. The outcome on earth could be Utopian. We could live in a world that is filled only with love. Hopefully we can reach this level before it is too late. If we manage to do this, our earth will progress and prosper. Our spirits will grow immeasurably. Many people will reach the master levels of enlightenment.

Can you imagine a world that lives, loves, and works together as one force in the universe?

Imagine and believe and it will exist. This world will be a wonderful and powerful place. Our spirits will feel love the way it was meant to be felt and be able to give love back freely, fully, and without reserve or question.

Picture a world with no wars, no hate, and no fear of any kind. Children would feel safe and have no need for protection from the horror that exists today. Men and women would be free to expand their territories and boundaries. Our spirits would then be liberated and grow at an accelerated rate. Judgments of any kind could not exist. People would be accepted for who they are spiritually, not physically or ethnically. In this world we would all be one. This is not an impossible goal to reach. It is possible and even easy to obtain if you follow the laws of God and Enlightenment:

**First: Do not take anybody's life. It is not your right.**

**Second: Help and give to people without expecting anything in return.**

**Third: Give love fully and without reserve or question.**

**Fourth: Ask God to enlarge or wealth and he will enlarge your spirit.**

**Fifth: Honor your intuition. Listen to and respect the voices inside yourself.**

**Sixth: Our spirit grows when our choices are positive in nature.**

**Seventh: Be aware of your lessons. Every morning ask what lesson will be sent to you.**

**Eighth: Protect Mother Earth.**

**Ninth: Take care of your body because you are the living circle of life.**

This is the level we, as human beings, are supposed to reach. This is what God wants for us. Right now it seems we are at a point where the world seems to be moving quicker and quicker and people feel that they can't keep up with it. No one has time to think, process or ponder the outcomes of their actions.

Now let me show you another possible future outcome for our world. Keep in mind we have the power to change the direction the world goes in. Any action that one part takes in will breed and equal reaction.

Currently our world is not headed in a positive direction. Terrorism strikes fear at the heart of our society. Wars are leading to more wars. This will bring us to only one place; a world clouded by negativity. Negativity grows on negativity. This can only lead us to total destruction.

Imagine now a world so barbaric that people feed off of each others' weaknesses. A world of hopelessness and despair, a world filled with fear, a world of poverty and hate. Picture the movie Mad Max" and imagine you are there. A world where basic staples like food and clean water are hard to come by. A world where you have to fight to stay alive. A world where people take from one another until there is nothing left to take.

It is right to fear this world. We are at a crossroads now. We are at a place where destiny has called us. We can change the path of the world by our actions. Be aware of the choices you make. Understand and follow the positive paths. Be your true self. One small action by an individual can start a chain reaction. Tell someone about this book. Help someone follow the positive path. They will then tell someone and the word will spread. By following our instincts, our intuition, we know what is right. We can change the outcome of the world.

If we follow our true path we will live in a world of peace and harmony. I do believe that in the end the positive will outweigh the negative. This is why I had to tell my story. Please tell others. God gave us this beautiful earth to live in. Let's not destroy it. Let's make it a positive plane of love as we were meant to.

The world will then fulfill its circle and go on and on for thousands of years. God meant for us to have a wondrous life. We want to have a wondrous life. I will say it one more time...

**Love is the only way.**

Made in the USA
Monee, IL
12 February 2023